Beautiful New Zealand

Photographs & Text by

PETER MORATH

FRPS

THE CAXTON PRESS
CHRISTCHURCH, NEW ZEALAND

Introduction

There are very few countries in the world of similar size that can compare with New Zealand for scenic variety.

In the North Island the white-sand beaches and the bays with their emerald waters provide gentle relief from the stark centre of the island with its mud pools, geysers and volcanoes.

Similarly in the South Island the bush-clad hills of the West Coast are far removed in appearance, though not in distance, from the golden tussock-covered expanses of the Mackenzie Country. However, both share a backdrop of clear lakes and towering snow-capped mountains.

One of the most lasting impressions gained by the traveller through this diverse land is of the clarity of its light and resulting brilliance of colour. While in a book of this size it is possible only to show a limited coverage of this diversity, one of the primary aims has been to convey that feeling of light and colour. In a world where atmospheric pollution is of increasing concern, New Zealand's clear, clean air is an asset of equal value to the magnificence of its scenery.

ISBN 0–908563–50–7

Printed at: THE CAXTON PRESS, CHRISTCHURCH, NEW ZEALAND

Contents

North Island pages 5–51

Northland 6–22

Bay of Islands 10–19

Auckland 23–29

West Coast 22, 33

East Coast 30, 31, 45

Central Districts 34–46

Rotorua 39–45

Wellington 47–51

South Island pages 52–112

Marlborough and Nelson 53–57

West Coast 58–63

Canterbury 64–85

Christchurch 68–72

Mount Cook 81–84

Otago 86–105

Queenstown 94–99

Dunedin 101–104

Southland and Fiordland 106–112

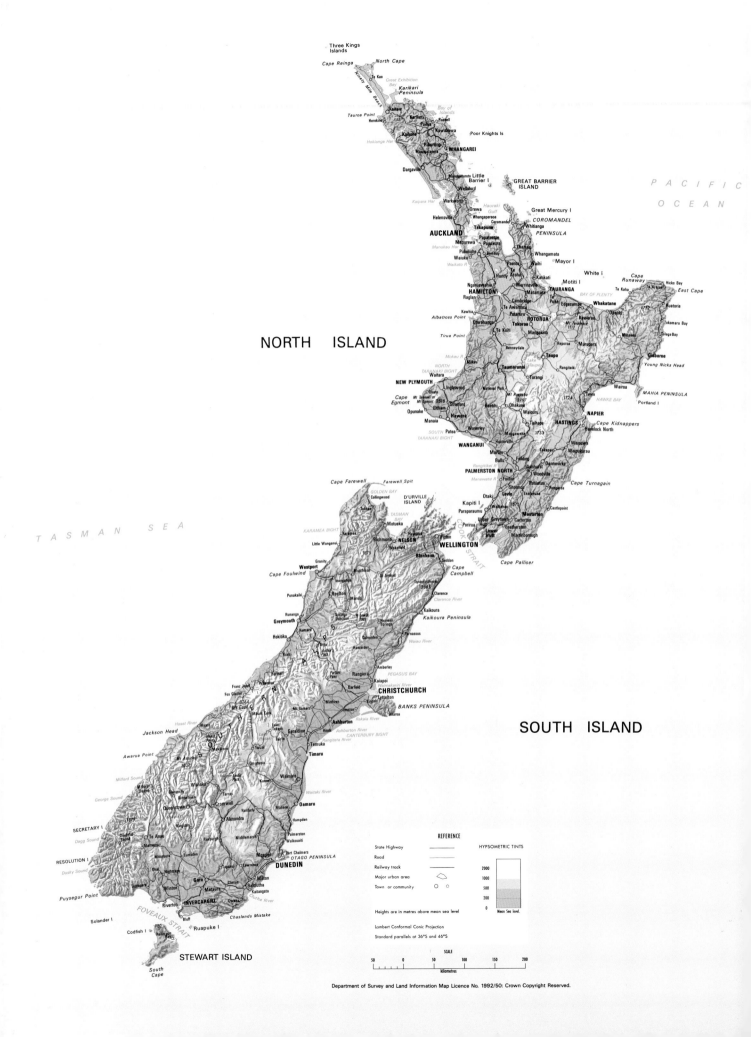

Three Kings
Islands

Cape Reinga   North Cape
             Kao
                   *Great Exhibition
                      Bay*
                   *Karikari
                    Peninsula*

Ninety Mile Beach

                         *Bay of
                          Islands*
Tauroa Point   Kerikeri   Russell
           Kaitaia   Paihia
            Herekino   Kawakawa
Hokianga Har Kaikohe
              Maungaturoto   Poor Knights Is
                Hikurangi
              WHANGAREI

       Dargaville   *Little
                   Maungaturoto   Barrier I*
              Wellsford   **GREAT BARRIER
                                             ISLAND**
Kaipara Har   Warkworth
                          Great Mercury I
           Helensville   Orewa
                     Whangaparaoa   Coromandel   *COROMANDEL
Manukau Har   **AUCKLAND**   Takapuna   Whitianga   PENINSULA*
              Manurewa   Papatoetoe
                Waiuku   Pukekohe Bombay   Thames   Whangamata
              Waikato R   Mercer   Whangamata   Mayor I
                                   Paeroa   Waihi
                     Ngaruawahia   Huntly   Te Aroha   Katikati   White I
                  HAMILTON   Morrinsville   Motiti I   *Cape
                      Raglan   Cambridge   **TAURANGA**   Runaway*
                                Te Awamutu   Te Puke   Edgecumbe   Hicks Bay
              Albatross Point   Putaruru   **Whakatane**   Te Araroa   *East Cape*
                                 Tokoroa   BAY OF PLENTY
                            Kihikihi   **ROTORUA**   Kawerau   Opotiki   Ruatoria
                  Tirua Point   Te Kuiti   Mt Tarawera
                              Mangakino   1111   Motu   Tokomaru Bay
                                     Reporoa   Murupara   Tolaga Bay
                  Mokau R   Mokau   Benneydale   Lake
                        NORTH   Taupo   *Taupo*   **Gisborne**
                   TARANAKI BIGHT   Taumarunui   Rangitaiki   *Young Nicks Head*
              Waitara   Turangi
       NEW PLYMOUTH   Inglewood   Wairoa
       *Cape   Mt Taranaki or   National Park   *MAHIA PENINSULA*
        Egmont* Mt Egmont 2518   Stratford   Mt Ruapehu   Portland I
                 Okato   Eltham   2797   Ohakune   *Hawke Bay*
              Opunake   Manaia   Hawera   Waiouru   **NAPIER**   *Cape Kidnappers*
                                                1724   Havelock North
                          Waverley   Patea   Taihape   **HASTINGS**
       *SOUTH   1733   Waipawa
        TARANAKI BIGHT*   **WANGANUI**   Hunterville   Takapau   Waipukurau
                           Marton   Ashhurst   Dannevirke
                      Bulls   Feilding   Woodville   *Cape Turnagain*
                    PALMERSTON NORTH   Foxton   Pahiatua
                    Rangitikei R   Shannon   Pongaroa
                    Manawatu R   Levin   1571   Castlepoint
                          Otaki   Waikanae   **Masterton**
                     Kapiti I   Paraparaumu   Upper   Carterton
                              Porirua   Hutt   Greytown   Featherston
                              WELLINGTON   Lower   Martinborough
                                           Hutt
                                    COOK STRAIT   *Cape Palliser*

NORTH   ISLAND

PACIFIC

OCEAN

Cape Farewell   Farewell Spit
            GOLDEN BAY
                   *D'URVILLE
                    ISLAND*
       Collingwood
                Takaka   *TASMAN
       KARAMEA BIGHT   BAY*
                Motueka
           Karamea   Richmond
                   Wakefield   **NELSON**
       Little Wanganui   Picton
                   1675   Blenheim   *COOK STRAIT*
                         Seddon
       Westport   Granity
       Cape Foulwind   *Cape
                      Murchison   Campbell*
              Reefton   Inangahua   Clarence
                   Maruia   *St Arnaud*   2061
       Punakaiki   Clarence
                         Springs   Lewis   *Clarence River*
              Runanga   Junction   Pass
       Greymouth   Kumara   Hanmer   Kaikoura
                         Springs   *Kaikoura Peninsula*
       Hokitika   Otira   Culverden
                      Parnassus
              Ross   Arthur's   *Waiau River*
                     Pass   Hawarden
                           Amberley
                        Rangiora   *PEGASUS BAY*
              Franz Josef   Waimakariri River   Kaiapoi
       Fox Glacier   Otira   Darfield   **CHRISTCHURCH**
       Jackson Head   3764   Springfield   Lyttelton
            Mt Cook   Mount Cook   *Rakaia River*   *BANKS PENINSULA*
                   Mt Somers   Methven   Akaroa
              Haast River   Fairlie   **Ashburton**
                         Hinds   *Ashburton River*
       Awarua Point   Haast   Geraldine   *Rangitata River*
                      Twizel   Temuka   *CANTERBURY BIGHT*
       Milford Sound   *SOUTHERN ALPS*   Pleasant   Point
              Mt Aspiring   Lake Tekapo   **Timaru**
                   3027   Lake Pukaki   *SOUTH   ISLAND*
       George Sound   Kurow
              Makarora   Wanaka   Waimate
       Mt Tutoko   Cromwell   Maheno   *Waitaki River*
       Doubtful Sound   Queenstown   Tarras   **Oamaru**
       SECRETARY I   Te Anau   Arrowtown   Ranfurly   Hampden
       Dagg Sound   1877   Kingston   Alexandra   Palmerston   *OTAGO PENINSULA*
                      Manapouri   Middlemarch
       RESOLUTION I   Mossburn   Ranfurly   Port Chalmers
       Dusky Sound   Lumsden   Waikouaiti   **DUNEDIN**
              Ohai   Nightcaps   Clinton   Milton   Mosgiel
       Puysegur Point   **Gore**   Lawrence   Balclutha
                      Mataura   Waikoikoi   Kaitangata   *Clutha River*
              Winton   Wyndham   Owaka
                   INVERCARGILL
       Solander I   Riverton   *FOVEAUX STRAIT*
                         Bluff   *Chaslands Mistake*
           Codfish I   Oban   Ruapuke I
              Halfmoon Bay

STEWART ISLAND

*South
Cape*

TASMAN   SEA

The North Island

He saw it in the distance, its whiteness stretching along the horizon; Kupe then knew that his long journey by canoe from Hawaiki 'the homeland' was almost accomplished. He named this country Aotearoa meaning 'Land of the Long White Cloud'. Such is one of the traditional beliefs held by some of the Maori people about the discovery of New Zealand.

The earliest inhabitants, the Moriori, are assumed to have come from east Polynesia around the tenth century AD. These Moa hunters lived mainly on the huge flightless bird which was found predominantly in the South Island. With the introduction of the kumara, a type of tropical sweet potato and with the near extinction of the Moa, the population gradually became concentrated in the North Island.

First sighted by the Dutch navigator Abel Tasman in 1642—and named 'Niew Zeeland' after his native province—it was not until Captain James Cook's arrival in 1769 that European sealers and whalers began to arrive and by 1814 the first missionaries had started to establish settlements, initially in the Bay of Islands region of Northland.

Today over two-thirds of the country's nearly three-and-a-half million inhabitants live in the North Island. This includes over ninety per cent of New Zealand's nine per cent Maori population. Northland's main industries are farming and tourism, although the country's largest oil refinery is at Marsden Point near Whangarei. The beautiful Bay of Islands is justly renowned as a boating and big-game fishing area and is Northland's main centre of tourism. It also has a thriving subtropical fruit-growing industry.

Auckland is the largest urban area in New Zealand and accommodates nearly one million inhabitants, over a quarter of the country's entire population. Situated between the Manukau and Waitemata Harbours, Auckland is a modern, fast-growing metropolis. Acknowledged as being the country's commercial capital, it is also known as the 'Capital of Polynesia', having the largest Polynesian population in the Pacific.

Many fine, scenic areas are within easy reach of Auckland. To the west are the Waitakares with bush-clad ranges and fine surfing beaches, while the lovely, island studded Hauraki Gulf is to the east. To the south-east, unspoiled native bush walks and white sand beaches shaded by pohutukawas combine to make the Coromandel peninsula a popular holiday area.

The Bay of Plenty's subtropical fruits are one of the many exports to pass through Tauranga's busy port at Mount Maunganui. This region established the large-scale production of kiwi fruit and is also well-known for its big-game fishing.

The Waikato is a major farming area and Hamilton, its provincial centre, is the country's largest inland city. It is situated on the Waikato River along which a series of power stations provides the main source of hydro-electricity generated within the North Island. This is also New Zealand's longest river. Hamilton's University of Waikato is one of four universities in the North Island, the others being Auckland, Massey at Palmerston North and Victoria University of Wellington.

The Volcanic Plateau is the island's most spectacular attraction. It includes the main thermal areas of Rotorua, Taupo and also Tongariro which was the country's first national park and is one of four in the North Island. Active volcanoes, geysers, mud pools, hot springs and geothermal development make this region unique in New Zealand. This central area of the island has a massive forestry industry, its timber products being major export earners.

Hawke's Bay, with its twin cities of Napier and Hastings, grows a large range of horticultural crops in its fertile soil. It is probably best known for its apples and for the more recent and highly acclaimed wine-making industry whose products, especially white wine, compare favourably with those of Europe.

The other major agricultural regions of the North Island are Manawatu and the Wairarapa, noted for their sheep farming and Taranaki, well known for its dairy products. Natural gas and synthetic fuel production are other important industries in Taranaki.

Wellington, the second largest urban area, has been New Zealand's capital since 1865, when the seat of government was transferred from Auckland. Situated on one of the world's most beautiful harbours it is the northern terminal of ferry services to and from the South Island.

Cape Reinga Lighthouse is within 5km of New Zealand's most northerly point. It has many visitors, most of whom travel by coach along the 90-Mile Beach from Kaitaia or Paihia.

Upper Cape Maria Van Diemen, to the south-west of the lighthouse, is one of only two places in New Zealand retaining names originally given to them by Abel Tasman. He named it after the wife of the Governor General of the Dutch East Indies who sponsored his expedition to find 'an unknown southern continent'.

Lower On this promontory at Cape Reinga grows a pohutukawa tree from which the spirits of the Maori departed are, according to tradition, said to set forth into the next life. Here the Tasman Sea and the Pacific Ocean meet, as can be clearly seen by the currents and by the different colours of the water.

A Northland farmer's wife, daughter and four-legged assistants prepare to drive a herd of Jersey cattle to fresh pastures between Hokianga and Dargaville.

This giant kauri tree is around twelve-hundred years old and 51m high. It grows in the Waipoua Forest which, together with the Trounson Kauri Park, is the last area of Northland where these trees can be seen in quantity. Timber and gum from the kauri created major industries in the last century.

Above Coopers Beach on Northland's Doubtless Bay is a magnificent stretch of sand joining two historic Maori pa sites. Cable Bay, Taipa and Mangonui are other popular holiday centres within a short distance. Pohutukawa trees are plentiful and are seen at their best around Christmas time.

Left Haruru Falls, sometimes known as Waitangi Falls, are on the Waitangi River and are reached by a short diversion from the Kerikeri to Waitangi highway. Like most waterfalls they are best seen after rain. Overlooking the falls is a large motor camp which has boating facilities.

In 1819 Kerikeri Basin was established as a mission station by The Rev. Samuel Marsden. The Mission House, now known as Kemp House, was built in 1822. The Stone Store, completed in 1835, still remains in business. The basin is a popular mooring for yachts.

Above Waitangi in the Bay of Islands is the site of the signing of the controversial Treaty of Waitangi which established this country as a colony and sought to create a partnership between the Crown and the Maori people. In this aerial view the bridge can be seen spanning the river to connect Waitangi with Paihia. Also visible is the 'Tui' ship museum.

Left The Maori meeting house at Waitangi has some fine examples of wall and ceiling decoration complemented by carving. These meeting houses are on marae, areas of Maori assembly, in many parts of the country. Most are in the north but there are also good examples in the South Island.

Above The mouth of the Waitangi River is another popular anchorage. Nearby is the Waitangi Hotel, one of the largest in the region. This view was taken at sunrise looking towards Paihia.

Right The Waitangi Treaty House, in front of which the document was signed in 1840, is open to the public. On the wide expanse of lawn, stretching to the water's edge, stands the flag pole used each year on the anniversary of the signing. Visitors come from many parts of the country for this event.

The reputation of the Bay of Islands as a 'paradise for boating' is confirmed in this aerial view of Opua. A vehicular ferry operates across the Veronica Channel, considerably reducing the travelling time to Russell.

Paihia, with plenty of hotel and motel accommodation, is one of the principal holiday resorts in the Bay of Islands. It is the headquarters of the main operator of coach and launch excursions in Northland. A passenger ferry service to and from Russell operates at frequent intervals throughout the day.

Russell is probably the gem among the Bay of Island's resorts. Steeped in history, it was the seat of government for a short time until 1841. It is hard to believe that this idyllic place once deserved its reputation as the 'Hell-hole of the Pacific', so numerous were its grog shops and houses of ill-repute.

Above Jacaranda trees, thriving in the mild climate, flower abundantly throughout Northland during the summer months. A fine example is seen here in one of the main streets in Russell.

Left Russell is one of the Bay's main big-game fishing centres. It is world renowned among followers of the sport who come mainly to catch the giant marlin. Here a proud angler is seen with his trophies.

Upper The 97km Cream Trip operates daily from Paihia and Russell. The launch cruises among the lovely islands of the Bay delivering supplies and mail. Passengers have many opportunities to observe bird and marine life.

Lower Roberton Island is one of the many delightful islands in the Bay. It is unusual in having two small tidal lagoons surrounded by short grass. These make it an ideal place for snorkeling, swimming and for picnic parties.

Upper Whangarei is the only city in Northland and is the regional centre. It has a busy port, a sheltered harbour and some fine beaches within easy reach. At Marsden Point is the country's main oil refinery. Laurie Hall Park seen here is in the city centre and is a colourful sight in the summer months.

Lower In recent years New Zealand has started to receive world recognition for the quality and distinction of its wines. Vineyards, such as this one in Northland, are increasing in number. The two main wine-producing regions are Hawke's Bay in the North Island and Marlborough in the South Island.

Whale Bay is 1.5km north of Matapouri on the lovely Tutukaka Coast. A short track from the road leads down to a delightful sandy beach. The dense bush, which includes nikau palms, provides plenty of shade.

Above Piha, about 40km from Auckland, is one of several surfing beaches on the North Island's west coast. To reach it one travels through the beautiful native bush of the Waitakere Ranges. Tree ferns grow in profusion, their graceful fronds forming a canopy over the road.

Left Kawau Island, on the Hauraki Gulf, is a mecca for yachting. Close to the Island's wharf stands Mansion House, once the home of Sir George Grey a former Governor and later Prime Minister. A short ferry service operates from near Warkworth and a longer one from Auckland.

Upper Auckland is the commercial capital of New Zealand, although the seat of government is in Wellington. A bustling modern metropolis, it is beautifully situated on the Waitemata Harbour with the symmetrical cone of Rangitoto Island as a backdrop. The Harbour Bridge carries the main highway north.

Lower Seen from the Ponsonby overbridge, streamers of light from fast moving vehicles follow the sweep of Auckland's Northern Motorway. The city has an extensive system of motorways which enables traffic to flow quickly and easily through central Auckland to the north, south and west, thus avoiding the congested inner streets.

Auckland Harbour Bridge is seen here from above the Northcote exit of the Northern Motorway.

Upper Hinemoa Park at Birkenhead overlooks the Auckland Harbour Bridge. Although close to the hustle of the city, it is a pleasant, quiet place to fish from the wharf, or simply to relax and watch the boats go by.

Lower Westhaven Marina with its hundreds of large yachts leaves little doubt of the interest of Aucklanders in sailing. It is one of several marinas in an area internationally known for the expertise of its yacht designers.

North Head at Devonport offers extensive views in all directions, encompassing Waitemata Harbour and some of the islands of the Hauraki Gulf. Looking towards the south-west, Devonport is in the foreground and Auckland city beyond.

Above Pohutukawas are plentiful throughout Auckland and its suburbs. These examples are at Devonport which is New Zealand's main naval base. A frequent ferry service operates to and from Auckland's Quay Street terminal.

Left Castor Bay is one of the many picturesque East Coast Bays on Auckland's North Shore. These stretch along most of the coastline from Cheltenham in the south to Long Bay in the north. Many have extensive grassed areas stretching from the road down to the beach and from most the distinctive shape of Rangitoto Island can be seen in the distance.

The colourful markets of Auckland provide amusement for young and old. Bargain hunters will find plenty to interest them and meals and snacks are available. *Upper* China Oriental Markets on Quay Street offer ethnic entertainment. *Right* Victoria Park Market is at the western end of Victoria Street.

Above The Coromandel Peninsula is a comfortable two hours' drive from Auckland. Kauri milling and gold prospecting were important industries in the last century. Plans to recommence mining are being constantly reviewed. The peninsula's main attractions are its forest areas and numerous sandy beaches. This view of the Tairua Estuary is seen from Mount Paku.

Left Hahei is north of Tairua on the east coast of Coromandel. From the north end of the beach a walking track leads to Cathedral Cave, a huge archway hollowed out of the limestone cliffs. The sheer-sided rock, Te Horo, stands a short distance away.

Upper Mount Maunganui in the Bay of Plenty is the site of a once heavily defended Maori pa. Below it stands the township on the north-eastern side of which is Ocean Beach, famous for its surf. On the south-western side is busy Port Tauranga, joined to the city of Tauranga by a toll bridge.

Lower Waikato with its provincial capital of Hamilton is renowned for its thoroughbred stud farms. Buyers come from all over the world to bid for horses whose later racing successes are legion. The stud seen here has every modern facility for stabling and breeding. Nearby is attractive Lake Karapiro with its hydro dam.

Above Poverty Bay in Gisborne is the site of the first landing in this country by Europeans. It was so named because a party from Captain Cook's *Endeavour* had a disagreement with the local Maori and returned aboard without supplies. The far headland was named Young Nick's Head after Cook's cabin boy who first sighted land.

Right The Taranaki coastline, about 70km north of New Plymouth, has some superb scenery. Colourful sandstone cliffs have been eroded by wind and sea to form sculptured islands and caverns. The White Cliffs Walkway near Tongaporutu provides some fine vantage points and on a clear day Mount Taranaki may be seen to the south.

Mount Taranaki, also known as Mount Egmont, is a symmetrical cone visible across much of the fertile dairy country of Taranaki. A dormant volcano, it is 2,518m in height and last erupted in about 1636. It is seen here from Lake Mangamahoe which serves the provincial capital of New Plymouth as a reservoir.

Upper This view shows the four main North Island volcanoes, Mount Taranaki in the foreground and the still active Ruapehu, Ngauruhoe and Tongariro on the horizon.

Lower Whakapapa is the largest of the ski-fields on Mount Ruapehu which, at 2,797m is the North Island's highest mountain. It has erupted many times.

Part of the Tongariro National Park, Mount Ngauruhoe which is 2,291m in height is the most active of the North Island's volcanoes. It erupts spectacularly every few years and steam is often seen rising from its crater. To the north can be seen Mount Tongariro which is the least active of the three mountains.

Above Taupo is New Zealand's largest lake and with its huge area of 619 sq/km it resembles a sea. This region is famous for its trout fishing and for the nearby thermal attractions and the fine golf course at Wairakei. Shown here is the marina near the town centre.

Right This beach, close to the centre of Taupo, is typical of the many fine boating and swimming beaches to be found within easy reach on the eastern side of the lake.

The Huka Falls north of Taupo are part of the Wairakei Park and are a spectacular sight. Here the mighty Waikato River is channelled into a gorge to form roaring rapids before plunging over the falls. The water is a brilliant turquoise and the surrounding hillsides are pleasantly wooded.

Above Rotorua's Bath House is beautifully situated in the colourful Government Gardens. It was built between 1906–7 in Elizabethan style and is one of the country's more impressive buildings. It now houses the city's museum and art gallery. Nearby are the Blue Baths and the Polynesian Pools.

Right The main attractions at Fairy and Rainbow Springs are the trout pools and delightful bush walks through many varieties of ferns. In the pools visitors can feed the very large and tame rainbow and brown trout. Other features are the deer park and a nocturnal aviary housing the native kiwi.

Above Close to Fairy and Rainbow Springs is the Gondola cable-car which transports visitors up Mount Ngongotaha. From there the view is extensive over both Lake Rotorua and the city. For the more adventurous there is a luge and an open chairlift.

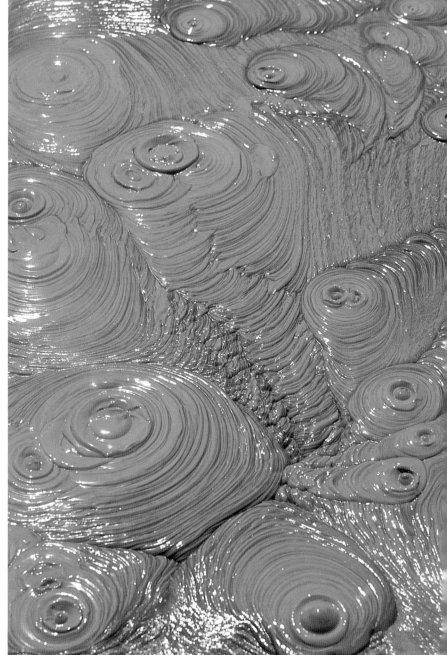

Right The boiling mud pools are one of the thermal fascinations of Rotorua. The plopping bubbles and jets of mud being shot high into the air form an ever-changing pattern of circles. Those shown here are at Whakarewarewa, but there are other good examples at Waiotapu.

The most impressive feature of the Waiotapu Thermal Area is the Lady Knox Geyser. This is persuaded to perform once a day by the introduction of soap into the vent. Other attractions include silica terraces and a Champagne Pool which effervesces when sand is thrown into it.

Above Seeing Maori in traditional dress is an experience that should not be missed. Much skill is required in the making of the intricately woven garments. This young lady welcomes visitors to Whakarewarewa, Rotorua's best-known thermal area. She is standing by the ornately carved archway entrance to the reserve.

Right While in Rotorua visitors have an opportunity of seeing Maori concert parties. These are held at both Ohinemutu and Whakarewarewa as well as at some of the hotels. Here a small group is seen dancing with pois in front of the meeting house at Ohinemutu.

Rotorua's main tourist attraction must surely be the Pohutu Geyser at Whakarewarewa. It is the largest in New Zealand and plays to a height of over 30m. Its playing is irregular, but activity by the nearby Prince of Wales Feathers geyser usually indicates that Pohutu is about to perform.

The Rotorua region has a rich variety of lakes, many of which are surrounded by unspoilt native bush. This aerial view of Lake Okataina shows Mount Tarawera in the distance. In 1886 this erupted and the explosion that followed was heard as far away as Christchurch: 153 people died and the famous Pink and White Terraces were lost forever.

Above Ohinemutu is an interesting Maori village around which the present city of Rotorua has grown. The extensive thermal activity is sometimes used for heating, washing and cooking. In front of Saint Faith's Church stands a bust of Queen Victoria presented in 1870 by the Queen's second son Prince Albert.

Right One of the principal attractions of the Hawke's Bay region is a conducted visit from Napier to Cape Kidnappers, site of the only mainland breeding colony of gannets in the world. Here the birds have little fear of humans, and nest close together in their hundreds on a flat area of the promontory. The fledgling gannets migrate to Australia, most returning about six years later to breed at their birth-place.

Palmerston North is the provincial centre of the rich farming region of Manawatu. The Square is its focal point and the gardens, ponds and fountains of this spacious area provide pleasant surroundings for some of the city's administrative buildings. Manawatu, particularly its Massey University, is well known for agricultural research.

Upper Wellington is New Zealand's capital city and the seat of government. It is acknowledged to have one of the most beautiful harbours in the world. An excellent place from which to see the city, both by day and night, is the lookout point on Mount Victoria which offers unrestricted views in all directions.

Lower The executive centre of Wellington's Parliament Buildings is colloquially known as the 'Beehive'. On the other side of Lambton Quay stands the old Government Building which was built in 1876 and is the second largest wooden building in the world, the largest being the Todaiji Temple in Japan.

47

This aerial view of Wellington shows most of the central city with its many modern high-rise buildings. In the middle distance is Oriental Bay, while on the far horizon can be seen the mountains of the Rimutaka Range.

Upper Wellington has a novel cable-car that winches passengers from Lambton Quay up to the pleasant hillside suburb of Kelburn. From Kelburn Park there are fine views of the central city and the harbour.

Lower Oriental Bay on Wellington's Marine Drive is a favourite place for the city's office workers to spend their lunchtime. There is a small sandy beach for bathing and the many Norfolk pines are an attractive feature.

Upper Wellington's extensive Botanic Gardens are a colourful sight for most of the year. Probably the most spectacular time to see them is early in October when the tulips are in bloom.

Lower This aerial view down the Hutt Valley shows the Hutt River, Lower Hutt, Petone and Wellington in the distance. On the far horizon, across Cook Strait, can be seen the Kaikoura mountains of the South Island.

The South Island

The morning mists parted and they saw it; fiery red in the light of the rising sun, its peak thrusting through a sea of cloud, up into the dark blue sky, while the rest of the earth lay in shadow. It was higher than anything they had ever seen and they named it Aorangi meaning 'cloud piercer'. Such may have been the impressions of the Maori people who first sighted the South Island's crowning landmark and New Zealand's highest mountain, later to be named Mount Cook.

By the time Captain James Cook had arrived only about five per cent of the Maori population remained in the south. The majority had moved to the warmer climate of the North Island.

European settlement followed a similar pattern to that in the north. Sealers and whalers arrived towards the end of the eighteenth century and the first mission station was established in 1840.

Large scale immigration from Britain began with the settlement of Nelson in 1842. Today about a third of New Zealand's population live in the South Island. Nelson, with the other most northerly province of Marlborough, has become a bountiful agricultural region with more sunshine than any other part of the country. Fruit, vines, hops, tobacco and also forests, thrive in the equable climate. Beaches of golden sand and the Marlborough Sounds, with their emerald waters, numerous peninsulas and bays, make an ideal holiday environment. Nelson has two of the South Island's eight national parks.

The beautiful West Coast has a very special, unspoiled grandeur. Its population is sparse and fishing, farming and forestry are the main industries, with some coal-mining near Greymouth, although in its heyday gold towns mushroomed—accompanied by saloons, gambling casinos and bordellos. Today, all that remains of this bustling activity are decaying ghost towns, swallowed by bush and fern. Dense native bush sweeps down to meet the pounding surf of the Tasman Sea; there is always a mountain backdrop and often a lake to mirror its image. Off-shore huge pillars of rock stand like sentinels where seals play and sea-birds wheel. Now it is peaceful in Westland, where once the Maori sought his greenstone and the pakeha his gold.

To the east, across the Main Divide which has twenty peaks over three thousand metres high, the scene changes dramatically. Bush gives way to the flat plains of Canterbury stretching further than the eye can see to meet the Pacific Ocean. This is the granary of New Zealand, but more than grain grows here. From the lush green of spring to the dry brown of summer this land supports sheep in their millions. There are fewer now than there once were, since markets have changed and farmers have had to face diversification. Now deer, angora goats and even llamas graze these vast plains. To the south, the Mackenzie basin has a large hydro-electric generating system using lakes linked by canals.

Christchurch, the provincial centre having over a quarter of a million inhabitants, is the South Island's largest urban area. With punts on its Avon River and magnificent gardens it is sometimes jokingly said to be 'more English than the English'. Close to the city's international airport are the Universities of Canterbury and Lincoln.

Otago is a province of contrasts, both in scenery and climate. The central region, with its superb mountains and lakes, has very warm summers and very cold winters. Frosts turn the leaves to gold but in the last century gold of a different kind lured thousands to this area. Fruit is grown on a large scale and Queenstown is the South Island's year-round tourist resort.

The green and fertile coastal lands are mainly agricultural and on the scenic Otago peninsula seals and penguins can be seen as can the only mainland nesting site in the world of the royal albatross. Built at the head of Otago Harbour stands Dunedin which, during the 1860 gold rush, became for a time the wealthiest and most populous city in New Zealand. The South Island's second largest city, known as the 'Edinburgh of the South', is noted for its grey stone, Victorian architecture and the University of Otago is a fine example of this style. Scottish traditions are still cherished today and the skirl of pipes often echoes around its hillsides.

Southland is another of New Zealand's major agricultural regions. Its high rainfall produces ideal grazing land even at the height of a dry summer. The scenery varies from rugged cliffs on the east coast, to rolling green pastures and bush-covered hillsides surrounding lakes Manapouri and Te Anau. Lake Manapouri's huge hydro-electric scheme, a tribute to the construction teams who worked in primitive and adverse conditions, provides power for the aluminium smelter at Tiwai Point near Bluff, a port well-known for its oysters. From there the mountains of lovely Stewart Island can be seen across Foveaux Strait.

Fiordland is one of the world's true, unspoiled wilderness areas. Milford Sound and the famous Milford Track are highlights of a visit to New Zealand.

Upper Picton on Queen Charlotte Sound is the South Island terminal of The Interislander ferry service across Cook Strait. The crossing usually takes under four hours and provides magnificent views of Wellington Harbour and the beautiful Marlborough Sounds. The ferry carries vehicles in addition to passengers and freight.

Lower This high-altitude aerial view shows the complex nature of the Marlborough Sounds' coastline. There is road access to many idyllic places in the region, but many of the bays and inlets can only be reached by boat. From both Picton and Havelock there are numerous launch excursions and fishing trips.

This scene near Ngakuta Bay is typical of the views from Queen Charlotte Drive. This scenic road, lined with tree ferns, runs from Picton to many lovely bush-surrounded bays which are ideal for swimming and picnics.

Kaiteriteri near Motueka is one of the most popular beaches in Nelson Province. The sand in this region is more golden than anywhere else in the country, and with its bush-fringed shores, the bay is perfect for bathing and boating.

Above Golden Bay at the north-western corner of Nelson Province is aptly named. Not only is the sand a warm golden colour, but the hours of sunshine are longer than in most other parts of the country. This aerial view shows sand patterns at Wainui Inlet on the western edge of the Abel Tasman National Park.

Left Tata Beach near Takaka in Golden Bay is another firm favourite for boating and bathing. About half an hour's drive away is Totaranui which is equally popular.

Upper New Zealand pioneered the large-scale commercial growing of kiwi fruit. They are produced mainly in the North Island but Nelson's sunny climate is suitable for growing many types of fruit and also tobacco. This kiwi fruit orchard is on the banks of the winding Takaka River which flows into Golden Bay.

Lower The Kaikoura coastline is noted for the rugged grandeur of its scenery. High, snow-capped peaks form a majestic backdrop to its pounding surf. The coastline has a large fur-seal colony and boats and helicopters operate whale-watching excursions on a regular basis throughout the year.

Upper The West Coast of the South Island is also noted for its wild, unspoiled scenery. These islands, known as the Motukiekie Rocks, are on the magnificent stretch of coastline between Greymouth and Westport.

Lower Knights Point in South Westland also offers superb views both north and south along the bush clad West Coast. A short distance further south the road swings inland to cross the Haast Pass into Central Otago.

The amazing Punakaiki Rocks are roughly mid-way between Greymouth and Westport. The name means 'pancake' and is derived from the flat stratified layers of limestone. In certain weather conditions blowholes shoot spray high into the air. The Punakaiki area is designated a national park and there are many fine native bush walks.

The West Coast has many beautiful lakes. The most notable of these is Lake Matheson near Fox Glacier township. In its placid waters are reflected Mounts Cook (3,753m) and Tasman (3,498m) the highest mountains in New Zealand.

Upper The rich, green pastures of the Franz Josef area of the West Coast are ideal for cattle rearing. Here a drover and his dogs guide a herd of Herefords along the main highway.

Lower No visit to the West Coast would be complete without a walk through the luxuriant native bush. The Minnehaha Track at Fox Glacier is close to the road and offers an easy and enjoyable introduction to bush walking.

Mounts Cook and Tasman are seen here from the small lake in the deer park at Fox Glacier township. Both Fox and Franz Josef townships are ideal centres from which to explore the area. Scenic flights operate on to both glaciers, the Fox and the Franz Josef and many of the lakes are within easy reach.

Upper Lewis Pass and Arthur's Pass connect the West Coast with Canterbury. Keas, the New Zealand mountain parrots, are often seen in both areas. These cheeky birds are inquisitive and destructive; items such as tramping boots and windscreen wipers if left unattended can be quickly destroyed.

Lower The Lewis Pass highway from the West Coast passes close to Hanmer Springs in North Canterbury. Famous for its hot, thermal pools, Hanmer has much to interest the visitor including golfing, pony-trekking, jet-boating and skiing. It also has many delightful forest walks which are especially enjoyable in autumn.

The Waimakariri is one of Canterbury's many shingle-bedded rivers. Here it is seen from above the gorge bridge with the Torlesse Range in the background. These rivers normally flow in multiple channels or 'braids', but after heavy rain the level rises rapidly and the water extends from bank to bank.

Above This rolling, sheep country is near Motunau in North Canterbury. The image of New Zealand is inevitably associated with sheep farming, sheep currently exceeding the human population by about seventeen to one. Changing markets have made farmers diversify, but sheep still play a major part in the country's economy.

Left A visit to a ewe sale is an interesting and amusing experience for the uninitiated. Hearing the stock agents, under the farmers' critical gaze, extolling the virtues of the animals provides an entertaining few hours. *Right* Many lambs are born during severe winter weather, requiring much care and attention from both farmers and ewes.

Left & Lower Christchurch is said to be the most English of New Zealand's cities. This impression is amply conveyed by the Avon River with its frequently passing punts and its banks lined with willows and flowering trees.

Upper Oxford and Cambridge Terraces curve gracefully around the Avon River. Autumn leaves drift lazily with the current, past the punts, towards the sea. This is seen from the roof of the city's highest building.

Victoria Square was completely redesigned in the late 1980s and has become one of Christchurch's main focal points. Close to the Avon and in its garden setting, it provides an ideal venue for many of the city's cultural and social events. The Town Hall and Parkroyal Hotel overlook the western side of the square.

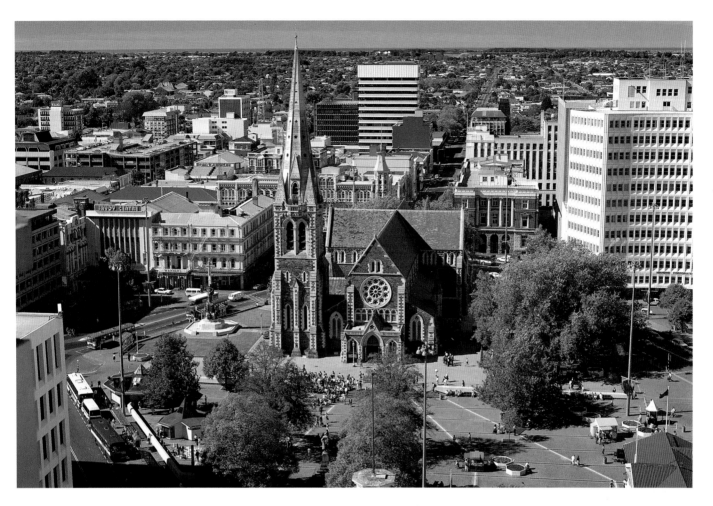

The Gothic architecture of Christchurch's Anglican Cathedral (*Upper*) and Arts Centre (*Lower*) emphasize the city's English atmosphere. Cathedral Square is a favourite place to relax or listen to the speakers while the popular weekend market at the Arts Centre adds colour to lively Worcester Boulevard with its cafés and entertainers.

Upper The citizens of Christchurch owe a great debt of gratitude to the foresight of the founding fathers for designating a vast area of the city centre as parkland. Known as Hagley Park this oasis now has beautiful, mature trees, sports fields, a golf course and an outstanding botanic garden.

Lower The wide estuary of the Avon and Heathcote Rivers provides a safe, shallow, though very tidal area for water sports. Wind-surfing and yachting are popular weekend recreations. In the background are the Port Hills, on the far side of which is Lyttelton, the busy port serving the Christchurch area.

Corsair Bay on Lyttelton Harbour is a favourite spot with Christchurch residents on warm summer weekends. It is in a sheltered position, protected by tall pine trees which also provide shade.

Lyttelton Harbour was formed in the crater of a long-extinct volcano. *Above* This aerial view shows Quail Island with the Port Hills, Lyttelton and Christchurch beyond. *Below* Seen from the Summit Road at sunrise, the Port Hills are to the left and the hills of Banks Peninsula to the right.

Akaroa Harbour on Banks Peninsula was also formed in the crater of a volcano. The settlement was founded originally in 1840 as the only French colony in the country and mainly intended as a whaling station, it soon passed into British hands. It still retains French street names although little else of the French connection remains.

Known as the 'Granary of New Zealand', the Canterbury Plains produce far more than cereal crops alone. Sheep and cattle are reared by the thousand and, in this aerial view near Ashburton, the yellow areas are fields of rape.

Upper New Zealand is a paradise for anglers. They come from all over the world to practise their skills on the wiley salmon and trout of the country's rivers and lakes. The Canterbury high-country is well endowed with fishing lakes; this scene shows Lake Sarah which is near Cass.

Lower Rugby football is the national sport of New Zealand. Its international team the 'All Blacks' has won great acclaim. The world-class players began their careers by playing for one of the many provincial or country teams, such as the one shown here playing a local game in Canterbury.

Lakes Grasmere (*Above*), Sarah and Pearson are three of Canterbury's lakes that provide good fishing. They are very near the main Arthur's Pass highway to the West Coast. In the background is the Craigieburn Range.

Mount Hutt is the highest and most popular of
Canterbury's many ski-fields. Equipment to make snow
artificially has been installed there and this enables the
skiing season to be considerably extended. Mount Hutt,
like several of the other ski-fields, is approximately one
hour's drive from Christchurch.

Upper The brilliant blue waters of Lake Tekapo form part of the region's hydro-electric generating scheme. The little 'Church of the Good Shepherd' shown here has a window framing a fine view down the lake. Nearby is a bronze statue honouring the sheep dogs of the Mackenzie country.

Lower When lupins were introduced to New Zealand it was not realized that they would become wild and thrive to the extent that they have. In the South Island vast areas are ablaze with colour in the summer months. Here they are seen against the background of part of Mount Sefton.

Above and Right Ski-planes operate from Mount Cook airfield and land on the glaciers. They also fly close to the towering splendours of the Southern Alps. Here, at sunset, the ice dome of Mount Tasman is seen against the shadow side of Mount Cook.

Above Glentanner Park near Mount Cook offers visitors a variety of recreational facilities. These include four-wheel drive excursions, horse-trekking and heli-skiing. Here, with the Tasman River valley in the background, a musterer from the nearby sheep station gathers his flock.

Above The Southern Alps offer the botanist much of interest. There are many species of rare alpine plants, some growing at very high altitudes. In late spring Mount Cook's Hooker Valley brings one variety within easy reach of the average walker. It is the mountain buttercup or Mount Cook lily (*Ranunculus Lyallii*).

The road connecting Mount Cook village with the main north-south highway skirts the full length of Lake Pukaki. Like Lake Tekapo, this is a brilliant shade of turquoise and the views looking towards the main divide are impressive.

Central Otago is known for the spectacular colourings of its trees in autumn. These are caused by the climate, particularly by its low night-time temperatures. Seen here is Glendhu Bay on Lake Wanaka.

Upper This aerial view of Albert Town shows the Clutha River near the beginning of its long journey from Lake Wanaka to the Otago coast near Balclutha south of Dunedin. A major gold prospecting area in the last century, the Clutha forms a vital part of the new Clyde Dam hydro-electric scheme.

Lower The secondary route from Wanaka to Queenstown is the highest public road in the country. It traverses the Crown Range and offers panoramic views at its southern end. It also passes through the lovely Cardrona Valley, shown here, which used to be another of the old gold prospecting areas.

The old suspension bridge over the Kawarau River near Arrowtown is one of the country's best-known locations for bungy jumping. The length of the drop is adjustable, some jumpers electing to touch the water on the initial bounce!

Above Arrowtown is steeped in the history of Central Otago gold-mining. This view shows part of the main street with some of the old, miners' cottages. The shopping area has been carefully developed, many of the old buildings being retained and new ones built in the style of the mining era.

Right In several places in New Zealand it is still possible to learn the art of gold-panning and even to find some gold. One such place is the Kawarau Gorge Mining Centre near Cromwell. Here it is also possible to see some of the old mining equipment.

Left & Upper Lake Hayes near Arrowtown is one of New Zealand's most photographed sights, especially when it is ablaze with autumn colour. Situated close to the main Queenstown highway, this small lake is a popular place for boating, fishing and picnics, or simply for feeding the ever-hungry duck population.

Lower Several high-country sheep stations receive visitors and show various interesting aspects of farm life including sheep dog demonstrations. The visits from Queenstown also include a pleasant launch or steamer trip to the opposite side of Lake Wakatipu where the stations are situated. Farm-style refreshments are often provided.

The secondary route from Arrowtown to Queenstown, via Arthur's Point, runs through lovely pastoral country. It also offers fine views of the northern end of The Remarkables Range, seen here both in spring and autumn.

There are opportunities for pony-trekking in Central Otago. Here riders are seen in the Arrow River valley. They are riding in the direction of Macetown and retracing the footsteps of the gold prospectors.

The Remarkables Range (2,342m) is a famous landmark of the Queenstown area. It has one of the highest ski-fields in the region and is seen here, across the Shotover valley, from Coronet Peak, itself a popular ski-field.

Several companies operate exciting jet-boat trips on the Shotover and Kawarau Rivers. Here is seen the Shotover near the Edith Cavell Bridge, a short distance from Arthur's Point. Some of these trips are combined with helicopter rides to provide a thrilling, action-packed experience in a relatively short time.

Upper A journey by steam train provides nostalgia for the older generation and a novel experience for younger people. The Kingston Flyer, with its immaculately polished locomotive, runs excursions from Kingston, which is at the southern extremity of the eastern arm of Lake Wakatipu.

Lower Queenstown is the South Island's major tourist resort. It offers the visitor an almost bewildering variety of all-year-round activities. Surrounded by rugged peaks, it is built on the hillsides overlooking beautiful Lake Wakatipu. Magnificent views are obtained from many windows of its hotels and motels.

A ride on Queenstown's Gondola cable-car provides good views of the town, the lake and The Remarkables Range beyond. The Skyline Restaurant enables visitors to dine whilst enjoying the view.

The vintage steamer the *T.S.S. Earnslaw* has sailed Lake Wakatipu since 1912 and is affectionately known as 'The Lady of the Lake'. For most of the year it provides three cruises a day of varying lengths.

Upper Mount Earnslaw (2,816m) with its distinctive peaks, forms a well-known landmark at the northern end of the western arm of Lake Wakatipu. It is seen here from the attractive lagoon at Glenorchy, which is at the end of the lake and is reached by an enjoyable, scenic drive from Queenstown.

Lower No drive to Glenorchy should be made without continuing another 18km to Paradise. This tranquil farming settlement overlooks the Dart River valley. Beyond the river, tower the peaks of eastern Fiordland. At Paradise there are pleasant areas of native bush, part of the Mount Aspiring National Park.

Upper Oamaru is the chief town of North Otago. Situated on the coast, its wide, tree-lined streets are flanked by fine buildings such as the Courthouse shown here. Many of these were constructed with the attractive local limestone which has also been used in constructing some of the country's most important buildings.

Lower The delightful seaside settlement of Karitane, 35km north of Dunedin, is a favourite place for bathing, boating and angling. Its fishing fleet is moored in the river which provides a convenient alternative to the magnificent ocean beach for swimming and water skiing. Across the Waikouaiti estuary is the Huriawa Peninsula.

Upper Dunedin is known as the 'Edinburgh of the South'. Its Scottish heritage and traditions are cherished and many of its street names confirm the origins of its founders. In this view along Stuart Street, the Law Courts are seen on the right with the railway station beyond.

Lower Port Chalmers in Otago Harbour is one of the South Island's principal ports. It has a large container terminal as well as a substantial fishing fleet. It was here that the first Dunedin settlers arrived and in 1882 the first trial cargo of frozen meat was shipped from this port to Britain.

This, the original section of Dunedin's University of Otago, was built in 1878. It was the country's first university and its architecture typifies the style used for several of the city's principal buildings.

Left Tunnel Beach is only a few kilometres south of Dunedin's suburb of St Clair. A pleasant, signposted walkway provides excellent views of rock formations, archways and cliffs being pounded by the surf.

Above Purakaunui Falls are near Owaka which is 31km south of Balclutha. This area is part of the Catlins district which has many reserves of native bush, bordered by beautiful beaches and cliffs worn by the sea to form caves.

Upper Te Anau is the largest lake in the South Island and is surrounded by dense native bush. The area has many attractions for visitors and the town is the region's main holiday centre. Te Anau is a convenient overnight resting place from which to visit Milford where accommodation is limited.

Lower Southland is one of the major sheep-farming areas of New Zealand. A fairly high rainfall produces lush green pastures—and much cleaner-looking sheep than in other regions with lower rainfall! This flock is seen, in the late evening light, at Te Anau Downs on the magnificently scenic road to Milford.

The road from Te Anau to Milford passes through the beautiful Eglinton valley. Here the green, glacier-fed waters of the Eglinton River are flanked by sheer mountains of the Fiordland National Park.

Milford Sound is one of New Zealand's best-known scenic highlights. The mountains lining the Sound rise almost vertically out of the water and this accentuates their already considerable height. Waterfalls cascade from high, hanging valleys, so completing a scene of great grandeur.

Above This winter, aerial view of Lake Quill shows the small gap on the far side through which the water flows to form the Sutherland Falls. These drop, in three stages, a total of over 580m and were once thought to be the world's highest falls.

Right No visitor to Milford should leave without having taken one of the frequent launch trips. These travel the full length of the Sound to the open sea, sailing close to the waterfalls. Passengers are given an informative commentary.

Mitre Peak (1,692m), though only one of many impressive mountains at Milford Sound, is certainly the most famous. Its pointed symmetry contrasts dramatically with the rounded shape of so many of Fiordland's peaks.

Bluff is the port which serves Invercargill, New Zealand's southernmost city. Bluff oysters are justly famous and part of the large fishing fleet is seen here in the harbour, the marker-floats making a colourful foreground.